Despite All Obstacles

La Salle and the Conquest of the Mississippi

MIKAYA PRESS

NEW YORK

BRIDGEWATER PUBLIC LIBRARY
15 SOUTH STREET
BRIDGEWATER, MA 02324

Editor: Stuart Waldman
Design: Lesley Ehlers Design

Copyright ©2001 Joan Elizabeth Goodman
Illustrations Copyright © Tom McNeely

All rights reserved. Published by Mikaya Press Inc.
No part of this publication may be reproduced in whole or in part or stored in a retrieval system,
or transmitted in any form or by any means, electronic, mechanical, photocopying, recording or
otherwise, without written permission of the publisher. For information regarding permission, write to:
Mikaya Press Inc., 12 Bedford Street, New York, N.Y. 10014.
Distributed in North America by: Firefly Books Ltd., 3680 Victoria Park Ave., Willowdale, Ontario, M2H3KI

Library of Congress Cataloging-in-Publication Data

Goodman, Joan E.
    Despite all obstacles: La Salle and the conquest of the Mississippi/ by Joan Elizabeth
Goodman; illustrated by Tom McNeely.
        p. cm.—(A great explorers book)
    Summary: A biography of the man who explored the St.Lawrence, Ohio, Illinois, and
Mississippi rivers, and who claimed America's heartland for King Louis XIV and France.
    ISBN 1-931414-01-7
        1. La Salle, Robert Cavelier, sieur de, 1643-1687—Juvenile literature. 2.
Explorers—Mississippi River—Biography—Juvenile literature. 3.
Explorers—France—Biography—Juvenile literature. 4. Mississippi River—Discovery and
exploration—French—Juvenile literature. 5. Mississippi River Valley—Discovery and
exploration—French—Juvenile literature. 6. Mississippi River Valley—History—To
1803—Juvenile literature. 7. Canada—History—To 1763 (New France)—Juvenile
literature. [1. La Salle, Robert Cavelier, sieur de, 1643-1687. 2 Explorers. 3.
Canada—Discovery and exploration—French. 4. Mississippi River—Discovery and
exploration.] 1. McNeely, Tom, ill. II. Title. III. Series.

F352. G66 2001
973.2'4'092—dc21
[B]
                                                                                    2001031732

Printed in China

Conquering the Mississippi

Keep the other side of this page open.
You can read about La Salle's travels and
follow them on the map at the same time.

$\longrightarrow$

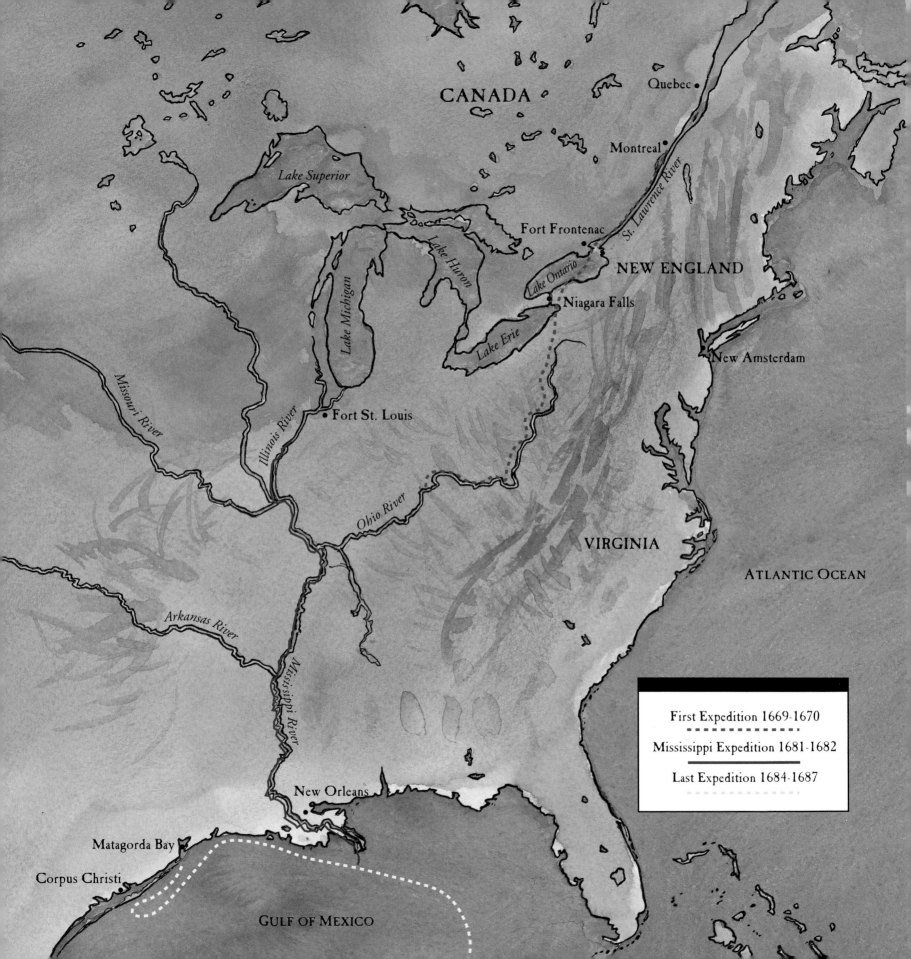

CANADA

Quebec

Montreal

Lake Superior

Fort Frontenac

St. Lawrence River

Lake Huron

Lake Michigan

Lake Ontario

NEW ENGLAND

Niagara Falls

Lake Erie

New Amsterdam

Missouri River

Illinois River

• Fort St. Louis

Ohio River

VIRGINIA

ATLANTIC OCEAN

Arkansas River

Mississippi River

New Orleans

Matagorda Bay

Corpus Christi

GULF OF MEXICO

First Expedition 1669-1670

Mississippi Expedition 1681-1682

Last Expedition 1684-1687

In Adversity he was never cast down

and always hoped with the help of heaven

to succeed in his enterprises

despite all the obstacles that rose against it.

CHRONICLE OF LA SALLE'S LAST EXPEDITION,
BY FATHER ANASTASIUS DOUAY

A GREAT EXPLORERS BOOK

Despite All Obstacles

La Salle and the Conquest of the Mississippi

By Joan Elizabeth Goodman

Illustrated by Tom McNeely

MIKAYA PRESS

NEW YORK

O N APRIL 9, 1682, René-Robert Cavelier, Sieur de La Salle, stood on a small rise of dry land where the great muddy Mississippi poured its waters into the Gulf of Mexico. He had changed his travel-worn shirt for a coat of brilliant red, kept especially for this moment of glory. By him stood his two closest companions: Nika, the Shawnee, and Henri de Tonty, his lieutenant. Father Zenobe Membré was there to bless their endeavor. Around them stood twenty-two Frenchmen and a small traveling village of Abenaki and Mohican who'd come with La Salle on the final leg of a journey begun, and interrupted, many times over the past five years.

Against incredible odds, La Salle had conquered the mystery of the mighty river that cut through the middle of America. Others had traveled it before him, but he was the first European to follow its course from its juncture with the Illinois River to its conclusion in the Gulf of Mexico. His mission was a complicated endeavor, every bit as difficult for its time as launching a space station is today. Only La Salle wasn't NASA. He was just one man. He alone negotiated with the French monarchy to get the necessary approval. He raised the funds, hired the men, and organized food, shelter, and supplies for the expedition.

At the mouth of the Mississippi, the men raised a tall, straight tree and carved on it the arms of Louis XIV, the dazzling Sun King, the greatest ruler France had ever known. La Salle stretched out his arms and claimed the entire Mississippi River basin from north to south, and from the Alleghany Mountains in the east to the Rockies in the west, for Louis and France. It was the huge midsection of the great North American continent, an area more than double the size of France.

Here was a gift fit for a great king. Spain had the riches of Mexico; England had the Atlantic coast; now France would have the heartland of America.†

EARLY ON René-Robert Cavelier showed the qualities that would help him overcome all obstacles in pursuit of his dream. He was born in 1643, second son of the wealthy merchant Jean Cavelier of Rouen, a trading city in the northwest corner of France.

René-Robert so outshone his brothers and sisters that his father gave him the estate of La Salle. At that time a man was defined by his property, so René-Robert became known as La Salle. At nine, they sent the bright young boy for the best education available in seventeenth-century France, a grammar school run by Jesuit priests.

One of the most demanding Catholic orders, the Jesuits brought Christianity to the far reaches of the world. Jesuit missionaries were the heroes of the day. Published accounts of their dramatic exploits captivated the bright, adventurous boy.

La Salle studied Latin, Greek, Hebrew, Arabic, Spanish, and Italian, as well as the sciences of the day, geography, astronomy, and navigation. He followed the strict rule of the monastery where study and prayer began at five in the morning and continued until nine at night.

Excelling at his studies, La Salle was invited to become a Jesuit when only seventeen. He knew it wasn't an easy life, but if he could travel to exotic lands it would be worth it. The Jesuit missions, particularly in China, were irresistible. La Salle weighed danger, excitement, and glory against a safe but dull merchant's life in Rouen and chose the Jesuits. He readily gave up his inheritance, taking the solemn vow of poverty as demanded by the order.

Four years later, having completed his studies, he was not on his way to the Far East. Instead, he was stuck in a small town, teaching young boys. He hadn't joined the order to waste his life in the backwaters of France. La Salle wrote to his superior in Rome, pleading with him to be sent to China.

This didn't work. The Jesuit fathers became concerned that the young man was too impatient and restless. When he was ordered back to school for more training, La Salle resigned from the order.

Still, he could not settle for a merchant's life. The New World beckoned. His elder brother, Jean, was a missionary priest in Montreal, and his cousins were growing prosperous in the Canadian fur trade. Canada was a far cry from China, yet a reasonable choice for a restless young man with no money. La Salle got on the next ship.

At that time North America was divided up by the major powers of Europe. The Dutch had a small but lucrative foothold in New Amsterdam (now New York). The English controlled the rest of the eastern coast from New England to Virginia. The Spanish ruled in the southwest, controlling Mexico and much of the Gulf Coast. The French had staked out eastern Canada as their territory.

Native populations had been deeply affected by this European invasion. The Spanish conquered and enslaved the native peoples, taking all the gold and silver they could find back to Spain. The English and Dutch were more intent on colonizing the New World. Sometimes that meant fighting the native peoples for land.

For eight full years, which is ever since my entrance into the Society, I have been desiring and petitioning with the greatest eagerness for admission to China. I have a very good training in mathematics. I have, too, a ready and retentive memory for languages.... I am large and robust of body....

LETTER FROM LA SALLE TO THE SUPERIOR GENERAL OF THE SOCIETY OF JESUS.

The French developed a different relationship with northern tribes. It was mutually beneficial and mostly peaceful, based on the trade in beaver pelts. This soft fur, made into felt hats, became enormously popular in France and the rest of Europe. Most prized were skins that had been worn by the natives because the stiff outer hairs were rubbed away, and they could be more easily worked into felt. The French traded metal goods, such as knives, axes, and kettles, as well as guns, cloth, and beads, for shiploads of the precious beaver pelts.

La Salle landed in Quebec and found it to be only a replica of French civilization. He hadn't suffered an ocean crossing to find himself in another provincial French town. He hurried on to Montreal.

The timing was excellent for an ambitious and energetic young man to arrive in Montreal. The French king, Louis XIV, had recently sent troops to subdue the fierce Iroquois. The most formidable of the North American natives, the Iroquois were a confederation of five tribes: Seneca, Mohawk, Oneida, Onondaga, and Cayuga. They supported each other in trade and warfare, and their territory covered a wide swath surrounding Lake Ontario and part of Lake Erie. Having depleted their own hunting grounds, the Iroquois warred against the French and their native allies, the Huron, for control of the north. Louis's troops checked their advance, although the Iroquois remained a force to be reckoned with.

The monks who ran the mission in Montreal welcomed the brother of Abbé Jean Cavelier. They saw in La Salle a likely young man with a religious background who could help them defend their mission. They gave La Salle several thousand acres at the edge of the wilderness to serve as a strategic outpost should the Iroquois renew hostilities.

La Salle's land was part of the endless wild forest of Canada. Here the merchant's son and the Jesuit scholar remade himself to fit the demands of the wilderness. Far from the ordered world of France, La Salle found adventure and a wonderful freedom he'd never known. He'd rejected the comforts of a merchant's life, the security and order of the monastery, and found his true home in the wilds of Canada.

La Salle studied the northern natives, the Iroquois and Huron. His facility with languages helped him communicate. La Salle admired their skills and quickly adopted their ways. He mastered the essential mode of transportation, paddling a canoe, and traded his boots for soft-soled moccasins that wouldn't rip the canoe's fragile skin of bark. He learned to orient himself in the woods, recognize animal tracks, and outwit the swarms of mosquitoes by greasing his body. Clearing his path with a hatchet and wearing buckskin to protect his legs, La Salle spent months in the wilderness, exploring its depths and training himself to endure hunger and exhaustion. He persisted throughout the severe Canadian winter, where bitter, relentless cold started in November and lasted until April. Snowfall, often six feet deep, smothered the land. La Salle dressed in bearskin and learned to walk on top of the snow with snowshoes.

Other men would have been content with the freedom and the wealth to be had trading trinkets and brandy to the natives for valuable furs—not La Salle. Being a trader in Canada was no more satisfying than being a merchant in France.

He saw in this wild place a passage to his dream of the Orient. The Iroquois spoke of a great, winding river leading to the sea. Perhaps this unknown river led west to the Pacific Ocean. Perhaps Canada would be his doorway to the Orient. He named his home after his dream, Lachine—China.

La Salle spent many hours with two Iroquois who wintered on his land, trying to learn their language and more about this mysterious river they called the Mississippi. During the long winter months he developed a plan to launch an expedition.

To raise money for men and equipment, he sold nearly all of his land back to the mission. The Iroquois agreed to guide him to Lake Ontario, and La Salle and twelve men set out on July 6, 1669, following the St. Lawrence River westward.

Their first objective was to get to the Ohio River, which the Iroquois told him led to the Mississippi. On August 2, they came to Lake Ontario and headed south. There La Salle encountered Senecas, tribal members of the Iroquois Nation. They urged him to come to their village. La Salle still needed someone to lead him to the Ohio. So he accepted their invitation in hopes of finding a guide.

Children welcomed La Salle with gifts of pumpkins and berries. Endless feasts, where dogs were slaughtered and roasted, honored La Salle and his men. Up until this time La Salle had seen only the more admirable side of the Iroquois he'd encountered—their strength, endurance, and courage. Now, another side revealed itself. A Seneca hunting party brought a young prisoner from another tribe to the village. He was tied to a stake and mercilessly tortured for six hours, while the tribal elders watched in satisfaction. At last, the Senecas cut their victim into pieces and ate him.

La Salle saw how the mood of the Senecas could easily shift. The French might be their next victims. He hadn't yet secured a guide, but it was time to move on.

For the life I am leading
has no other attraction for
me than that of honor and
the more danger and
difficulty there is in
undertakings of this sort
the more worthy of honor
I think they are.

➤➤·◄

LETTER FROM LA SALLE
TO A FRIEND

On September 24, past the roar of Niagara Falls, at the farthest western point of Lake Ontario, they came to a friendlier Iroquois village. Here La Salle bartered for a guide, Nika, a prisoner from the Shawnee tribe.

Although their relationship began as that of master and slave, it quickly evolved into one of mutual respect and trust. They matched each other in physical strength and endurance. La Salle's self-described "solitary nature," which often put off his French associates, was readily acceptable to a Native American. For seventeen years they were inseparable.

La Salle had always walked ahead of his men clearing the path. Now Nika walked by his side. Word by word, each taught the other his own language. Within a few weeks they'd learned enough to converse easily.

La Salle and his men wintered away from the windy lake and continued their search in the spring. Eventually they found the westward flowing Ohio River. From afar it looked wide and deep, an easy passage to their goal. But the Ohio proved to be shallow and impossible to navigate. The men struggled along, most often carrying their loaded canoes over knife-like rocks and through snake-infested waters.

The misery of the disheartened men went unnoticed by La Salle. One of his great failings as a leader was in not recognizing the needs of his men. Undaunted by obstacles and ignoring his own suffering, La Salle could push on forever to achieve his goal. He didn't realize that his men couldn't, and wouldn't. One night they slipped away, taking with them all the food and equipment. Only Nika remained. Without him, La Salle would have perished in the winter wilderness. The two walked nearly a thousand miles through snow and ice back to Montreal—a trek that would have killed most men.

All the money he'd invested in the expedition was gone, with nothing to show for it. But that wouldn't keep him from trying to find the Mississippi and follow it to the sea.

Over the next three years La Salle traveled and traded extensively around the Great Lakes, going as far as the tip of Lake Michigan, where Chicago stands today. He needed to recoup the losses from his first expedition and put together more funds for the exploration of the Mississippi. During this time Louis Joliet and Father Jacques Marquette found and explored the Mississippi far enough to establish that it did not run to the western sea. It flowed south, probably into the Gulf of Mexico.

With this discovery, La Salle's hope of finding a new route to China had ended, but not his need to explore. The Mississippi held out the promise of a grander dream.

By this time, through his own travels and what he'd learned from other traders, he'd gotten a much broader picture of North America. South and west of the virgin forests of Canada, the source of the precious beaver skins, stretched vast, fertile prairie lands. Besides being perfect for cultivation, these plains teemed with herds of elk, deer, and the strange, shaggy buffalo. Here was enough game to feed all of Europe. Perhaps this was where the French would find precious gems and metals. Most important of all, the Great Lakes connected the wealth of the central plains to Canada. Goods and men could travel back and forth easily to this heartland.

Oxen, cows, stags, does
and turkeys are found in
greater number than
elsewhere. There are wide
prairies....A settler
would not have to spend
ten years in cutting and
burning trees; on the
very day of his arrival
he could put his plow
into the ground.

THE JOURNAL OF THE VOYAGE
OF MARQUETTE AND JOLIET

La Salle began to formulate a plan as large as the continent. He envisioned the expansion of New France first westward a thousand miles to the plains, then south another thousand miles along the Mississippi to the warm waters of the Gulf of Mexico. Here trade with Europe could continue throughout the winter, unlike at Quebec, which was icebound from November through April.

Far more ambitious than exploring a river, this plan would increase France's holdings in the New World by thousands of miles. There was one problem: the king of France. La Salle knew that Louis XIV opposed expansion of the French colony in North America. A small New France enabled him to keep a tight rein on his overseas subjects. La Salle had to go cautiously to get the permission necessary to proceed. He would present only the part of his plan most likely to find favor with Louis XIV.

Trading his buckskins for satin and lace, La Salle set sail with Nika for France in 1674.

The court of Louis XIV was as full of snares and snags as the densest forest of North America. He may have chosen the wilderness as his home, but La Salle's Jesuit training never left him, and he was quite capable of negotiating in the civilized world. His clarity of mind and speech impressed the powerful finance minister, Jean Colbert. Perhaps most convincing was that La Salle didn't ask the king for money.

Through Colbert, La Salle got the king's backing to build and operate a permanent fort and trading post on Lake Ontario and for further explorations in the region. He was raised to the rank of nobility. This royal support enabled La Salle to get substantial loans from the merchants of Paris and Rouen.

However, Louis's support was limited. He had given Sieur de La Salle a license to trade and to explore more of the North American territory. That didn't mean that Louis had changed his mind about expanding the French colony.

When La Salle returned to North America, he built Fort Frontenac where the St. Lawrence River flowed into Lake Ontario. This massive, stone fortress, named after the governor of Canada, housed a small civilian population and as many soldiers as those garrisoned at Montreal. It was the gateway to the Great Lakes and a critical point from which to expand into the central plains.

Next, he had to make sure of the cooperation and friendship of the Great Lakes tribes as well as those of the plains. La Salle spent the next two years seeking out the tribes along the shores of Lake Ontario, gaining their confidence and trade.

With Fort Frontenac up and running successfully, La Salle returned to France in 1677. This time he asked not only for permission to explore the entire length of the Mississippi but also for a license to build and garrison forts along the way to protect his interests.

I cannot help, Monseigneur, recommending to you the **Sieur de La Salle**, who is about to go to France and who is a man of intelligence and ability, more capable than anybody else I know here to accomplish every kind of enterprise and discovery that may be entrusted to him.

❧➤ ➤❧

LETTER FROM FRONTENAC
TO COLBERT

Perhaps hoping for discoveries of gold or silver in the new territories or developing trade in buffalo hides, the king gave La Salle his license. There was no mention of colonies—and there was a catch: the license was only valid for five years.

La Salle wasn't concerned about the king's limitations. It was a heady time for the merchant's son of Rouen. He was convinced that the success of his explorations would win Louis's approval of La Salle's grand plan for the expansion of New France down the Mississippi to the Gulf.

La Salle returned to Canada in 1678 with Henri de Tonty, the man who would help make this dream a reality. Losing a hand in battle had ended Tonty's military career, but in no way diminished the man. Tonty used his metal hand as a formidable weapon in battle. His courage won great respect among the North American tribes and was matched by his deep loyalty and commitment to La Salle. Although La Salle never asked more from any man than he asked of himself, most men fell far short of his energy, endurance, and determination. Henri de Tonty never let him down.

Before proceeding with the exploration of the Mississippi, La Salle needed to establish a Great Lakes trading operation to pay for his expeditions. First he'd build a fort and trading post at Niagara Falls. Above the Falls he'd build a ship nearly as large as an oceangoing vessel to carry furs through all the Great Lakes. These furs would finance his expedition. Until this time only canoes and small barges had traveled the Lakes. To build a ship of this size and complexity in the Canadian wilderness was a vast undertaking, bordering on madness.

Tonty kept the French shipwrights working throughout the winter, in spite of harsh weather and the constant Iroquois threat. La Salle went back to Montreal to raise money for necessary supplies. By summer the impossible had been accomplished—the beautiful *Griffon* was launched. La Salle returned to Niagara to supervise her maiden voyage through the Great Lakes.

On her way back to Niagara, with a hold full of precious furs, the *Griffon* sank to the bottom of Lake Michigan. Undaunted, La Salle carried on. He walked, with Nika, a thousand miles back to Montreal to raise more money and start over.

Over the next four years, La Salle faced one setback after another while relentlessly pursuing his dream. He traveled from the Great Lakes to the Illinois River, building forts, making alliances with the different tribes, and collecting a fortune in furs. Yet each success was quickly followed by a crushing defeat.

His men, working in miserable and dangerous conditions, deserted. Feeling no loyalty toward the aloof La Salle, they stole what they could. Some destroyed the very forts they'd built with their own hands. La Salle became more in debt than ever.

But he would not be defeated, not even by his most deadly opponents, the Iroquois, who were once again on the warpath. La Salle's enterprise had encroached on their trading territory. If the Iroquois attacked La Salle directly, they would have drawn reprisals from the French army. Instead, they launched a campaign of terror and cannibalism against the tribes who traded with him. La Salle's new allies, the Illinois, were their first victims.

La Salle realized that none of his plans could go forward until he could stop the Iroquois threat. He decided to unite the tribes of the Great Lakes and central plains. Together, they'd be strong enough to defend themselves and to protect his forts and furs against the fury of the Iroquois. Unity would not come easily. These tribes were small, isolated communities, speaking diverse languages, and many had been at war with each other.

La Salle invited the various tribes to a great council. Included were Abenaki and Mohican from far away New England, survivors of wars with the British. If his diplomacy at the French court was admirable, La Salle's ability to win over the tribes was truly inspired. He stood tall in the smoke-filled lodge of a Miami chieftain, surrounded by the tribal elders and young warriors.

La Salle spoke in the language of the Miami. He presented himself as the reincarnation of one of the Miami's greatest chiefs, Ouabicolcata, saying that he'd come back from the dead to lead them. Old griefs and quarrels were to be buried and forgotten. He brought forth a feast to celebrate Ouabicolcata's return.

La Salle continued, urging the tribes to stand together, and together they would survive and prosper. He punctuated his speech with lavish gifts of tobacco, knives, axes, blankets, and, finally, guns. In perhaps his finest hour, La Salle won them over.

"You ought to live at peace with your neighbors....You have an interest in preserving them; since if the Iroquois destroy them, they will next destroy you."

LA SALLE'S SPEECH TO THE GREAT COUNCIL.

Only one year was left on La Salle's license to explore the Mississippi and build forts there. The groundwork for the expedition was in place. It was time to go.

On December 19, 1681, La Salle assembled enough men and provisions for their journey. Before the expedition could get under way, five of the newly hired men deserted. La Salle immediately turned to the Abenaki and Mohican, asking them to act as hunters and, if need be, as fighters. The Indians agreed as long as they could bring their wives to cook and carry. Some brought their children as well.

Delayed by so many obstacles over the years, the great journey began at last. It started with the men hitched to the sledges like oxen, dragging their supplies over the frozen ground and down the icebound Illinois River.

On February 6, 1682, where the Illinois River empties into the Mississippi, the ice ended. They stopped long enough to build elm-bark canoes to carry the whole expedition. Eighteen Abenakis and Mohicans with their ten wives and three children, Nika, twenty-three Frenchmen, including Henri de Tonty, the priest Father Zenobe Membré (who would write the story of their journey), and René-Robert Cavelier, Sieur de La Salle, set out to find and follow the great, swift river to the sea.

After all the work and danger of the past years, the beginning of their journey must have seemed a placid dream. The current carried them along the clear water. Fifteen miles later they reached the juncture where the muddy Missouri roars into the Mississippi. Big chunks of land torn from western riverbanks and uprooted trees rushed around them in a swirling torrent. For ten miles the two rivers fought with each other before becoming the one great muddy river.

The weather grew mild. They drifted through lush grasslands, abundant with game and fine stands of trees. A hundred miles downstream they passed the mouth of the Ohio River, pouring its clear stream into the Mississippi.

Following the river's twists and turns ever southward, they left the northern winter behind. A southern spring warmed the air and greened the land around them.

Nearing a village of the Arkansas tribe on March 12, they heard war whoops and drumbeats. Under cover of fog, they landed on the shore opposite the Arkansas and hurriedly constructed a fort. When the fog lifted, the amazed Arkansas saw the log walls and a large group of strangers, some with white skin and beards. Perhaps the French were the first white men they'd ever seen.

La Salle held aloft the long pipe, called a calumet, the symbol of peace amongst all native peoples. A small group of Arkansas came forward in their canoes and invited the French to rest in their village. La Salle brought presents of tobacco and trade goods. The Arkansas honored and feasted the French, eager to make an alliance with these well-armed strangers in order to use them to fight their own enemies.

On March 14, La Salle planted a large cross, carved with the arms of Louis XIV, in the center of the Arkansas village. He told the elders that from now on they would be under the protection of the greatest king of Europe. Whether or not the Arkansas understood that they now belonged to France, Father Zenobe wrote that they showed "great joy!"

Two Arkansas guides took the expedition downriver toward their allies, the Taensa. On March 20, La Salle sent Tonty and Father Zenobe, laden with gifts, across a swamp to a small inland lake. There they came to a native town unlike any they'd seen before. The Taensa lived in houses made of mud and straw, covered with finely woven mats. The chief's house was forty feet square, with high walls and a domed roof. It faced the equally grand temple of the sun god, on which was perched three carved eagles facing east to greet the dawn.

Seated on a bed with three of his wives, the chief welcomed his visitors. Sixty elders dressed in white robes surrounded him. The chief, after expressing his pleasure at the arrival of the French, said that he would come to meet La Salle.

The next day, the chief's deputy came early to clear a path and line it with cane matting. The tambour and the women's song heralded the chief's arrival. A procession, headed by two men carrying fans of white feathers, led the white-robed chief to La Salle.

La Salle greeted the chief respectfully and brought forth more presents. In turn, the chief lavished provisions upon the French. He also gave them some of the white robes, woven from mulberry bark. By the time the Taensa chief departed, La Salle had made a friend and won an ally.

Not every tribe welcomed La Salle and his men. On April 2, the Quinipissa responded to the offered calumet with a shower of arrows. La Salle moved his men quickly past them to avoid bloodshed. Several miles further south, they came to the

The column was erected by M. de La Salle, who standing near it, said, with a loud voice, in French: "In the name of the most high, mighty, invincible and victorious Prince Louis the Great, by the Grace of God King of France ... I have taken, and now do take, in the name of his Majesty and of his successors to the crown, possession of this country of Louisiana."

→»⋅«←

AN ACCOUNT OF THE TAKING POSSESSION OF LOUISIANA BY JACQUES DE LA METAIRIE

village of the Tangibao. A few days before the fierce Quinipissa had attacked the village. Now, only burnt cabins and piles of corpses remained.

La Salle pushed forward, arriving on April 6 at a point where the great river divides into three channels. The salt smell of sea filled the warm air. La Salle sent one canoe down each deep, brackish channel. The water grew increasingly salty until they all came to the open sea! Here was the Gulf of Mexico. All the labor, the heartbreak, the cost, and the bloodshed of thirteen years had brought La Salle to this immensely satisfying conclusion.

This would be a fitting place to end La Salle's story. He had finally proven to himself, and the world, that his dream could be a reality. An all-year port for New France would open the whole Mississippi Valley and Canada. He stood on the brink of seeing, at last, his brilliant vision for New France come true. The whole rich, beautiful land he'd traveled now belonged to France. Frenchmen could trade the harsh, perilous existence of Canada for the plenty of the Mississippi Valley. He named this land, from the Gulf to Canada, Louisiana, in honor of his king.

When Louis learned the news of La Salle's success, he said: "I am persuaded that the Sieur de La Salle's discovery is quite useless."

The king had never shared La Salle's dreams for North America. This was especially true at that moment as France was being threatened by its archenemy, Spain. Louis's concern always was that his country reign supreme in Europe. He would not dilute France's strength by sending men and arms to the New World.

Without the king's support for his discovery, La Salle was ruined. It didn't matter that the native confederation was succeeding, and many tribes were flocking to his new Fort St. Louis on the Illinois. When La Salle's five-year license to maintain forts and trade expired, the governor of Canada seized all of his forts and goods. In one stroke, he was destitute.

The dream may have been shattered, but the dreamer had a will of iron. Sieur de La Salle simply could not give up. He had never before accepted defeat. He would not now. In the past he'd swayed the mighty ministers of France in favor of his plans. Surely he'd be able to do so again. Once more, he and Nika crossed the Atlantic to plead his case before the king.

La Salle proposed building a fort at the mouth of the Mississippi River from which he would attack the Spanish silver mines in Mexico. He promised the king that he would raise an army of nineteen thousand warriors from his confederation of native nations. He asked only for an armed ship, two hundred French soldiers, guns, ammunition, and supplies for six months. In return La Salle would capture Spain's main source of silver, simultaneously striking a blow at France's enemy and enriching the king. He knew this plan would win Louis's heart and fooled himself into believing it possible.

In reality, the mouth of the Mississippi was twelve hundred miles from the Spanish silver mines. La Salle could not possibly raise an army of nineteen thousand native warriors. Even if they existed, they certainly wouldn't and couldn't follow him on a European-style campaign against the Spaniards.

La Salle would also be commanding without his trusted lieutenant, Tonty, who had remained in North America, trying both to maintain the native alliances and protect what he could of La Salle's interests. Instead, La Salle would bring his brother, Abbé Jean Cavelier, and two nephews, Colin and Moranget. Not any of them equaled Tonty, and Moranget was a born troublemaker.

Perhaps the greatest flaw in La Salle's scheme was his own inexperience in organizing and commanding large numbers of men. La Salle was not a general. Alone, he had accomplished the impossible, but he wasn't able to inspire men to remain under his command. La Salle was a brilliant individual who'd successfully transformed himself many times; no doubt he felt that leading an army would come to him as easily as learning Greek, or snowshoeing across the frozen north woods. It wouldn't.

La Salle's plan was the desperate scheme of a desperate man. The past fourteen years of work had amounted to less than nothing. This was his last chance to establish a fort on the Mississippi and to rise from the ashes.

On April 14, 1684, Louis XIV gave La Salle his blessing.

They embarked on July 24, 1684. La Salle commanded four ships, overloaded with soldiers, colonists, artisans, and supplies, but not enough water. By the time they reached Santo Domingo, on September 27, 1684, over fifty of the men, including La Salle, were deathly ill. One of the ships had been captured by Spanish pirates, and a number of men had deserted.

When La Salle recovered, he pushed on to find the mouth of the Mississippi. They entered the Gulf of Mexico guided by inaccurate maps and an inexperienced pilot. According to La Salle's limited information, their first landfall was off the west coast of Florida. In fact the ships were already west of the Mississippi River.

How could they have missed the muddy river rushing into the clear blue Gulf? Easily. La Salle had last seen the mouth of the Mississippi from the land. The Mississippi divides not only into the three channels he'd explored, but again and again. From the Gulf it looked just like the rest of the waterlogged coastline.

So they continued westward, through January, as far as Corpus Christi in what is now Texas. There it became clear, by the southern trend of the coast, that they'd overshot the Mississippi by hundreds of miles.

La Salle ordered the ships to turn back. At Matagorda Bay, he felt sure he was close to a river that would lead him to the Mississippi. He landed and built a fort. Over the next two years, La Salle led parties of men through swamps and deserts in search of his river. He never found it. Meanwhile, disease, bad water, and hostile natives killed most of the colonists.

By the close of 1686, of the one hundred and eighty French who'd landed at Matagorda Bay, only forty survived. When their last remaining ship sank and left them completely cut off from Santo Domingo, La Salle decided that their only hope of survival depended on walking three thousand miles back to Canada for help.

On their own La Salle and Nika might have successfully made the trip. Unfortunately, La Salle brought most of the men with him. Several raged against La Salle for getting them into this predicament, and they hated his nephew Moranget. The miserable trek through marsh and thicket drove their anger to the point of murder.

The assassins' first victims were Moranget and the innocent Nika, bludgeoned to death at a hunting camp while they slept.

The next day, March 20, 1687, when La Salle approached the camp, his men shot him point blank, in the face. He fell dead on the ground. They stripped him naked and left the Sieur de La Salle to the wolves and vultures.

His passion, courage, and indomitable will helped La Salle make a mark on a vast wilderness. His aloof and unyielding nature undermined the pursuit of his dream and led to his ignoble death. It was a cruel, undeserved end for the man who had dreamed a great future for New France.

Epilogue

Twelve years later, Louis XIV revised his position on settlements in the New World. In 1699, permission was granted to Pierre le Moyne, Sieur d'Iberville, to found a colony at the mouth of the Mississippi. Once across the Atlantic, he hugged the Gulf Coast to the mouth of the great river. He wasn't certain it was the Mississippi until he came to a native village, near what is now New Orleans. There he was shown a letter written by Tonty fourteen years before, when he had traveled to the mouth of the Mississippi looking for his friend and commander, René-Robert Cavelier, Sieur de La Salle.

It would be many years before La Salle's dream came true. New Orleans became the capital of Louisiana and a vital port for France. However, the string of fortified colonies and the bustling trade moving up and down the river that La Salle envisioned didn't materialize. Goods might move down the river, but going against the current upriver was nearly impossible.

In 1803, Napoleon sold Louisiana to the fledgling United States for fifteen million dollars. Thomas Jefferson paid a hefty price to secure the Gulf port, and what was then mostly wilderness.

In 1810, with the arrival of the steamboat, travel upriver became feasible.

The mighty Mississippi joined the north and south. A horde of colonists settled the fertile valley. At last, La Salle's dream was realized, not for France, but for America. †

This nineteenth-century map of the United States shows the vast Louisiana territory in yellow.

Authors Note

Many of the sources quoted in this book were written by men hired to join La Salle's expedition as chroniclers. Their job was to keep an account of all that was seen and discovered on the journeys. Priests often filled this role.

The accounts were official documents, meant for the Canadian governor, the ministers of France, and King Louis XIV. However, the exploits were so exciting, the chronicles often found a wider audience. Maybe they inspired the next generation of explorers just as the Jesuit missionaries' stories had captivated La Salle.

Index

Credits

CORBIS: p. 45
Tom McNeely: pp. 5, 8-9, 11, 14, 18-19, 22-23, 26, 29, 30, 33, 37, 40-41, 43